How I Learned English
The Story of a Brave Mexican Girl

Paula Massadas Pereira

This book is dedicated to those who left their countries behind to embark on a new journey.

My name is Claudia Sánchez. I am from Mexico. When I was a child, I helped my parents at our farm in Jalisco state, Mexico. We had cows, horses, chickens, and a big corn field. My family has been farming for many generations.

Claudia's family farm on a sunny day.

I spent my childhood going to school in the mornings and helping my parents in the afternoons. Life was not easy, but I enjoyed myself playing with my family and friends. We all relaxed at night.

After a busy day in the fields, my dad liked to talk to his farmer friends on our porch. My mom cooked delicious, authentic Mexican food. Her tortillas were the best! My sister Dolores and I liked watching her. Mom is a great cook. The neighbors came to our porch many times a week to eat her food.

Claudia and Dolores helping their mom make tortillas.

As I grew older, my parents did not want to see me working in the corn fields. When I was 20 years old, they sent me to Dallas, Texas, to live the American dream. It was my first experience away from home, from my dear family and friends.

The city was huge, and it had people from all over the world. It was very different from my little village in Jalisco. The first months were very difficult. Before I left my hometown, my parents gave me enough money for three months. I did not know anyone in Dallas. I had no job, and I needed to find work fast.

On the day I arrived, I rented a small apartment close to downtown. It was very small. It had a bathroom, a tiny kitchen, and enough space for a bed and a desk. It was okay.

The first few weeks were very hard. I spent hours walking around looking for work. I looked for jobs at restaurants, schools, pharmacies, and many other places. I saw many Hispanics on the streets. Weeks later, I was happy to find a job at a Mexican market.

The big city of Dallas at dusk.

At the market, I met many nice people from all over Latin America. We had fun, and we worked hard organizing the fruits and vegetables. During our lunch breaks, we talked about life in our countries. We all shared similar life experiences. I really liked talking to them. They reminded me of my loved ones in Mexico.

María worked with me. She had beautiful long hair and she was always smiling. She moved to the United States from El Salvador one year before I moved from Mexico. I felt like she understood me. She was my best friend.

All my friends wanted to learn English, but it was very hard because we spoke Spanish all the time. Most of the store customers also spoke Spanish, but at least I felt like I was home.

Claudia and María waiting for customers at the market.

Two years later, I was working at the same place. I was okay there, but I did not want to work so many hours per day, six days a week, for the rest of my life. The work at the market was intense, just like in my parents' farm in Mexico. So, little by little I realized that I needed to change a few things in my life. One day, after a long day of work, I opened my mailbox and saw a flyer advertising classes at a local community college.

The flyer that changed Claudia's life.

I asked my boss for a day off to visit the college and find out about English classes. I finished high school in Mexico, and this was my first time visiting a college. The college was so clean and big. I was amazed to see so many students my age. I saw students in the classrooms, at the cafeteria, and in the library. They were everywhere! They had free access to computers to do their homework. I felt like I belonged there. I wanted to be one of them. On the same morning, I talked to a counselor, and she suggested that I take English as a Second Language classes. These were very basic English classes to help me read and write. I decided to take classes in the fall.

The college campus.

When the fall semester started, my life changed a lot. I had a new backpack, new books, pencils, and notebooks. I was very excited. I had to make some sacrifices, but I was thrilled. Now I had to work and go to college. I got up at 5:30 a.m., went to work in the mornings, and went to college in the afternoons. I spent my nights studying at the library.

The first semester was hard. I learned many new words in English. I also started to pay attention to how people pronounced words. I did not know how to talk like them, but I tried. My teachers were proud of me. They knew I wanted to learn. I got good grades in all my classes.

After the first semester, I continued to study. I took more classes to learn English. I started going to the computer lab to improve my writing, listening, and speaking skills. This helped me a lot. I spent one hour, three times a week, watching videos.

College students learning new verb tenses in the classroom.

A few months later, my teachers told me to speak English as much as possible. It was time to look for another job because I needed to practice my new language. I looked for a job at the college library because I liked it there. It was quiet and it had many interesting books.

When I got the job at the library, I knew I had to leave my job at the market. I was sad to leave all my friends from the market but I knew it was the right decision. I was a little afraid to work at the library because my vocabulary was not very good.

Claudia checking out books at the library.

Every morning, I had breakfast with my friends from the market before I went to work at the library. I continued to speak Spanish with them. They wanted to know about college life. I always smiled when I talked about college. I loved it!

My best friend, María, was a nurse in her country. She loved to help patients at the hospital where she worked. She wanted to become a nurse in Dallas. She needed to learn English to work as a nurse in the United States. After I talked to her about my college experiences, she decided to take classes too.

Friends enjoying a nice breakfast.

At the library, I organized books and watched my supervisors helping students. I asked them about words I did not know, and they always explained them to me. After one semester working at the library, I started to help students at the circulation counter. I scanned their library cards and the books they wanted to borrow. I was happy to speak English. It was a big challenge for me.

Sometimes, I had to work for a few minutes by myself. When the phone rang, I was afraid to answer it. I was very nervous. Many times, it was hard to understand what people were saying. I usually asked them to repeat what they said. I had a little notebook with standard answers I heard from my supervisors.

Claudia nervous about answering the phone.

I continued to take classes for two more years. I finished all the English courses I needed to take. To finish college, I took several classes in other subjects. I learned a lot about the world. I actively participated in my classes. I always raised my hand when I had a question. Some lessons were very hard. I had to pay close attention. I took biology, history, sociology, art, psychology, chemistry, philosophy, and many other classes.

I made many new friends, and I studied with them twice a week. My English was much better. I was not so afraid to talk anymore. I continued to make a few mistakes, but that was normal. I sometimes had to think about the past tense of the verbs, but I still communicated well. My teachers thought I was an excellent student. They thought I learned fast.

At the library, my supervisors gave me more responsibilities because they thought I was doing very well. I was a dedicated employee, and I was excited to be working at a place I really liked. I learned how people interact in the United States. I learned a lot about American culture.

Studying at the library with her college friends.

Three years after I started college, I graduated with very good grades. I was really happy! I knew what I wanted to do. I wanted to continue my education. I wanted to go to the local university to become an English teacher.

When I was 25 years old, I got my degree in English. On the day of my graduation party, I cried tears of joy. I celebrated with all my friends from college. María and all my dear friends from the market were also there. They were inspired by my story. Many of them wanted to go to college and learn English. They were very proud of me.

Claudia surrounded by friends during her unforgettable graduation day.

The day after my graduation, I went on a trip to my hometown and took my diploma with me. I wanted to show it to my family. I wanted to share my happiness with them. They were the reason behind my success.

My parents invited all my friends to celebrate. My mother cooked all my favorite foods, and my sister Dolores, Uncle Miguel, and Aunt Sílvia played my favorite mariachi songs. Everyone from my village wanted to give me a hug and congratulate me. My house was beautifully decorated. It had a big sign that read, "Welcome Home, Claudita!"

This was one of the best moments of my life. Before dinner, I showed my diploma to all my friends and family and thanked everyone for their support and love. I was very emotional and happy.

Dolores, Miguel, and Sílvia surprising Claudia with Mariachi songs.

When I came back to the United States, I got a job at a school. I helped many children learn English. I played many games with them, took them on small trips, and sang songs with them. They learned fast. I was very proud of them.

I love my life in Dallas, but I go back to visit my country at least once a year. Sometimes, I just need to see my family and have a good time with them. I am a true Mexican, and I love to be part of our traditions. I need to see my loved ones and participate in all of our family gatherings. In the end, the United States has my admiration and Mexico has my heart.

I hope my story can be an inspiration to all my fellow immigrants who came to the United States for the American dream.

Truly,

Claudia

Claudia thankful for the wonderful opportunities she had in the United States.

READING COMPREHENSION:

1) Where was Claudia Sanchez born?

2) Why did she move to Dallas, Texas?

3) Where did she first find work?

4) How did she communicate with her family while she was living in Dallas?

5) How were her English skills when she first arrived in the United States?

6) What did she think about her college when she first visited it?

7) Did she study hard?

8) How did she improve her English?

9) What happened to Claudia after she finished school? Did she find work?

10) Does she like living in the United States? Why?

11) How does your life compare to Claudia's?

12) How do you think Claudia succeeded? What qualities does she have that make her successful?

13) What are the biggest challenges immigrants face when moving to another country?

14) What is your life story?

VOCABULARY:

What are the definitions of the following words?

Access:

Amaze:

Belong:

Counter:

Customer:

Dusk:

Employee:

Flyer:

Gathering:

Huge:

Intense:

Porch:

Realize:

Standard:

Suggest:

Thrill:

Tiny:

Trip:

ABOUT THE AUTHOR

My name is Paula, and I wrote this book because I also struggled to learn English. I was born and raised in Rio de Janeiro, Brazil. I moved to the United States with my family when I was nineteen years old. I studied English in Brazil for nine years, but when I immigrated I realized that I needed to learn a lot more. I took English as a Second Language classes at ABC Adult School and Cerritos Community College. I also worked at the college library to interact with native speakers. I loved the library but I was terrified.

Nine years after my arrival, I obtained my master's degree in library and information science. I am now a librarian. I teach students library services and resources that will help them be successful in their academic and personal pursuits.

Learning a new language is hard, but it is achievable. If I did it, you can do it too!

Made in United States
North Haven, CT
19 May 2022

19310221R00020